MW00562080

I HAVE NOTHING TO SAY
ABOUT FIRE

ALSO BY MARJORIE SAISER

I HAVE NOTHING TO SAY
ABOUT FIRE

■ ■ ■

Poems

Marjorie Saiser

The Backwaters Press

© 2016 by Marjorie Saiser
All rights reserved. Except for brief quotations in critical articles or reviews, no part of this book may be reproduced in any manner without prior written permission from the publisher:

The Backwaters Press
1124 Pacific St., #8392
Omaha, NE, 68108
(402) 451-4052

The Backwaters Press

Published 2016 by The Backwaters Press

Saiser, Marjorie
       I Have Nothing to Say about Fire / Marjorie Saiser.
       ISBN 978-1-935218-39-5 (pb)
       Library of Congress Control Number: 2015959450

Front cover photo by Calvin D. Stilen
Cover design, interior design, and typesetting by Steve Foley
The text of this book is set in Adobe Caslon Pro.

First Edition

Printed in the United States of America
This book is printed on recycled, acid-free paper.

For Don, again

CONTENTS

II. Through This Thin Wall

III. Bright Kite Over the Horizon

I HAVE NOTHING TO SAY
ABOUT FIRE

I.

A LARK SINGS SOMEWHERE CLOSE

I Have Nothing to Say About Fire

I have nothing to say about fire
except my father could build one
his hands moved logs into place
his hands with scars I would recognize

anywhere I have nothing to say about hands
except his were old and
good I have nothing to say about good

they are right and left hands: *good* and *lucky*
I could say
guilt because my sister on some other side of the world
to the left or right of lucky

is biting her lip tasting blood she may be
lying on a floor thinking of pain
I have nothing to say because I have said it
and am lucky, undeserving, I who

did not earn did not choose did not merit.
I have nothing to say, time to say it,
people to listen. I have everything.

I Meant to Write of My Sister's Pain

but I was at the cabin with my friends. We wanted
to ride the golf cart down to the lake

so we fit our bodies in, three in front, three in back, our arms
around one another to keep from falling off.

Our pale light ran ahead of us on the road, the moon
rose as if it meant to be a gold coin on a vast plain,

and when we walked on the beach, the moon, having no
competition, made our shadows long and thin moving across sand.

The water was warm with ribbons of cool on our legs;
we floated, our faces and knees very small islands.

On the return, the curves in the road were hard to see. One of us
started to sing *You look like my friend even though we are at war.*

We joined in the words we knew and hummed and faked.
One of us began *When we've been there ten thousand years*

and one of us began the silence that followed:
only the hum of the golf cart, only the hum of the moon.

Smaller

When the smaller bird
dive-bombs a hawk, I see

it maneuvers to be above,
never below.
It throws its body at the enemy,

hurls what it has at the order of things,
does what it can against thievery,

dives at the wingspan it should fear,
not with talons but with thin ordinary feet,
hits the hawk,

which merely shivers and flies on
but there is an interval, a chink,
when the smaller

flings its all,
and the single-minded body of power,
for an instant, gives.

Forgive Me, Distant Wars

> *Forgive me, distant wars, for bringing flowers home.*
> —Wislawa Szymborska

Small boy, forgive me.
Breaking news tells of you,
and the big man who

scraped your skin,
cursed you, stuffed your body
into a file drawer, slammed it

shut on your cries.
I cannot forget your murder—
but I do forget.

I look up a recipe.
I search my cabinets
for sugar, for salt.

Your mouth jammed
against some part of your leg—
how could he do that—

how could this world
let him?

Child, stranger,
you cried out and went silent.
I have watched sunrise happen
on the Santa Rita Mountains.

I have walked in the shade,
a breeze flapping my scarf. I have
laughed with friends a thousand days.

What I Think My Father Loved

He signed up,
walked in a line to the troop carrier.

Newly shorn. New scratchy uniform.
I think he loved the green of the island

and he loved the ocean. He told me he watched
a native man float like a log in the surf. My father

on the shore, working, looking up
from time to time to see him floating,

rising on a wave, white foam
lapping over, dissolving, reforming.

When the man came out of the water,
my father spoke to him, asking

how to float and ride like that.
The answer: Don't tell the ocean what to do.

When my father's work was done,
the beach was dark. I imagine him

wading in, a barely visible line of foam
coming toward him like a greeting.

I imagine him, farm boy from a different
hemisphere, his feet leaving the bottom,

his body lying back in the bed of the water,
ocean lifting and turning,

ocean holding him loosely,
rolling him.

He Gives Me All Continents

My father sits in the circle of men around the table
after dinner on Christmas Day,

the women having gone off
to look at quilts, to spread them out

in the spare bedroom and discuss calico.
The men stay. I stay,

leaning on my father's shoulder while Uncle Joe,
home on leave, passes around photographs:

uncle to uncle and into my father's hands,
the hands I had earlier been playing with,

flopping one of them, placing my fingertips
into the depressions left by infection.

My father's hands take their turn
holding the photos: airplanes on the tarmac

and next, a photo of women whose naked
breasts hang like slack fruit.

Uncle Joe is laughing, not the loud laughing
of the card game, but a lower snickering,

until he remembers me, the child. He looks
to my father and begins to apologize. My father does

not hide the pictures,
the women, their breasts, the shining skin.

He gives citizenship. He gives the body, all continents.
No, he says, not snickering,

and his quiet voice changes my uncle's face:
No, she can see this.

I.

Storms damage my father's pear trees,
petals falling to the ground with the hailstones.

II.

He walks under the broken trees
in the cancer days.
His steps falter, he pretends
my mother has his hand, she is his love.
The days spin by so fast and so slow.

III.

He is young, carrying a fishing pole, then he is
a soldier crossing the equator,
the gray water, the waves.
The captain's voice:
With every turn of the screw
we are deeper and deeper into enemy waters.

In the darkness he digs his foxhole on the beach,
waits in his helmet,
the bullets, the screams.
In New Guinea, paradise of green,
he gets jungle rot under the leather of his boots,

sprays his skin with DDT.
He is a cook in a tent, he pares and peels and chops;
he comes home different and the same, his wife

waiting with the child.
She will not leave the town,
so he builds there;
jack of all trades, he says, master of none.
After his day of work measuring, nailing, laying blocks,

farmers come to his house, tell him
the project they have for him: remodel a kitchen,
add a bedroom, a bath.
He has all the work he needs,
all he can handle.
The spring storms break his pear trees

but they bear fruit.
He likes that. They may be stunted and
split, but the fruit is good.

The Story, Part of It

The story, part of it, is that
the tractor was parked, running,
at the top of the hill, and
my sister Jennie, ten years old, climbed
up and took a seat at the wheel. The story,

part of it, is that my father worked on something
attached behind the tractor, the digger or the chain
perhaps; the story does not tell all. It tells
what he said to Jennie, his instruction; it tells
what he said into the fierce wind blowing that day,
the roar of the wind and the roar of the tractor.

He said *Whatever you do, don't step on the clutch.*
The wind took his words, flipped and turned them,
gusted them even as it gusted everything,
even as it tossed the ends of the red scarf Jennie wore,
flapping it out and back, out and back. Jennie
heard him say *Step on the clutch* and she did.
The tractor lurched down the hill like an animal

freed. The story, part of it, tells how the tractor
rolled, gaining, how Jennie stood steadfast
on the clutch, hanging onto the wheel, her hair
and her red scarf flying with the speed of it, how
the tractor sped down the slope until it
hit the barbed wire fence at the bottom,
broke through and rolled over,
how she flew off, and the clutch engaged and
killed the engine. Everything was at that second

silent from the roaring, and Jennie was
face down on the grass, alive, but he, my father,
thought she was dead.

And years later when my father was dying, I called
Jennie. *You'd better come,* I said. She arrived
at the hospital and I met her at the main door
to show her through the maze, the halls,
to my father's last room. We turned the turn
and could see him ahead. No longer
a man at work. Or rather a man doing
the new work of dying. He sat in the bed, tubes
into the skin of the backs of his hands.
He looked up and caught

sight of her, of us, and then he did what
Jennie cannot explain, get over, understand,
make sense of: he put his hand over his eyes;
he looked down at the floor while we came to him.
The story, part of it, is that Jennie cannot let go of this.
She told me: *It's what he's always done—*
he did not want to see me, to look at me.
No, I told her. *No, it was to keep from crying.*

It Does Not Have to Be Worth the Dying

I wrote about my father's death
before he died, a recognition,
not a premonition. I had been at
the cabin, resting
on an inner tube in the lake or
lying on a towel in the shade,
listening to the motor boats and
shouts of children and the slow
stirring of leaves in the cottonwoods
near the deck. I'd been sleeping all night
with the windows open. I'd been walking
barefoot in hot sand, standing
in the kitchen in my swimsuit, fixing
sandwiches for kids. Sunday,
on the ride home, I watched cornfields
roll by. Suddenly against the slope of a field
I saw my father's head, large, his eyes
closed, and I knew what it would be
for me when he died, when that love went
out, that form gone, closed, done.
I wrote, tears running, cheeks wet,
wrote and wrote as if to stop it
or keep it. Later my friend said
one should never write about that,
your father dying; you invite these
things to happen. But I knew she was
wrong. The leaves turn and churn
slowly all night in the cottonwoods
in August. The lake is deep under
the sky whether or not we wake

and hear waves slapping the sand,
whether or not we rouse up and see
a patch of light the moon makes,
a shimmer floating on the water.

Hands

My father's hands pick up the small stove and carry it from the room, orange flames rising to his face. I follow him into the yard where he sets the stove down and turns to me. He squats, holds out his arms. His eyebrows are singed, his hands burned.

My father's hands milk the cow. I stand beside him and lean my head on his shoulder while he milks. His shoulder moves with the motion of his hands. The milk is a white foam; it rises slowly. There is the faint smell of his shirt and the sound of milk squirting into the pail.

I am old enough to do a little work. I get into the pickup and my father drives. The foundation has been dug; concrete blocks wait in stacks. My father's right hand holds a trowel, his left a block. We have sandwiches from our cooler and ice water in a jug. We'll take a rest, my father says, and he lies back on the grass, puts his cap over his face. A cardinal sings two notes again and again in the cottonwood. I look for a red bird in the green leaves but do not find it.

My father throws up his hands. He cannot understand why I cry. I am in high school, came home for lunch, and refuse to return. I don't know how to say I am ugly and nothing is right, not my homemade jumper, not my wrong shoes.

I am pregnant, I am unmarried, it is time to tell my father. It is very late, he is in bed, not sleeping, my mother beside him, saying nothing. I hate crying. When I get away from here, I will never cry again. My father's voice in the dark is kind. I tell him what I must.

2.

His hands lie on top the sheets. The nurses have given him his bath.
His hands remain a working man's hands but are the color hands
become when they have not been in the sun.

I stand with my son and my daughter in a prairie cemetery.
Everything is done: the minister, flowers, the ropes lowering the
casket. Most of the people are gone. A lark sings somewhere close.
We three have our arms linked. A man is walking toward us, a friend
of my father's. On one side my daughter, on one side my son, I wait
for this one more condolence, this one more hand to shake. The wind
moves my hair, brushes down the blades of the grass.

I Am a Good Liar

Since my father is dead I can make him up, something I like to do
and something he didn't do much. He cautioned me against lying.
I was a good liar and he may have thought about that while he was
working, sawing two-by-fours or tossing tools into the back of the
truck after the job. I make them up, my father and mother needling
one another to quit smoking, and one of them threw down

the whole carton on the kitchen floor and each walked around it
for weeks—I'm making it up, the green carton on the tiles—weeks
of quitting smoking, no talking except a few words related to work.
I doubt if she took to writing notes but I could be wrong. I know
he didn't write notes because he hardly ever wrote anything; he
was ashamed of his handwriting, even his signature on a check.
Somebody had made him ashamed. There is one surviving

sticky note on which he wrote a message. He wanted my mother
to call me after my divorce. He couldn't use the telephone, had the
same trouble I do, calling somebody: they might be busy or the words
might not come out right. God knows why he couldn't call but he
wanted me to be called, wanted me to feel supported and loved and
cherished. I am making this up. He wanted my mother to call and
she wouldn't and didn't. I don't know why I can't make up her life as
fast as I make up his. He asked *Did you call her?*

and she went on frying hamburgers, saying *What* in that way a person
says *What* just to keep from answering. He was taking off his work
boots, peeling off his sweaty socks and shirt, washing his hands and
arms in the basin, splashing water over his face. She said *No I did not.
What would you want me to say?* She knew what he wanted her to say.
She didn't look at him; she turned the meat, grease misting up and
falling down onto the clean white stove. He didn't repeat what he

wanted her to tell me but later that night after supper and before
the chair in front of the cop show and the late news, he got a pad of
paper from the drawer (I said it was a sticky note, but I lied) and a
ballpoint and he wrote without punctuation *tell her we love her and
we hope Paul will come back some day*. My father could not believe it,
the child going with the father after the divorce, could not think of a
child being lost to the mother, could not fathom how I could stand it,
Paul gone.

He left the yellow note on the round oak table and went to
bed, turned on his side, drew the sheet up to his chin, closed his
eyes. Years later my mother gave me the yellow square with his
handwriting. Maybe she had called me, I think she did, and gave
me a message of sorts, I don't remember and can't make it up. But I
remember she handed me the yellow square. This was

remarkable. She didn't have to. She knew he was my favorite; I
think she knew that, and she, like me, did not like to be second
best, but she gave me what he had written. He didn't know if she
would call me; he may have thought about that while working, while
hammering a nail into wood, striking it hard, striking extra times
after the nail was already driven in.

She Gives Me the Watch off Her Arm

my mother wants me to
go to college

the closest she has ever been
is this
the dorm

her father had needed her
to dig the potatoes
and load them into burlap bags

but here she is
leaving her daughter

on the campus in the city time to go
we are at the desk
the clerk is wide-

eyed when my mother
asks her if she will
take an out-of-town check

if the need arises
if something comes up
so my girl will have money

even I know
this isn't going to happen
this check-cashing

a clerk helping me with money
but miracle of miracles
the clerk says nothing

and I say nothing
and my mother feels better
we go to the parking lot

old glasses thick graying hair
she is wearing a man's shirt
has to get back to the job

we stand beside her Ford and it is
here she undoes the buckle of the watch
and holds it out to me

my father's watch
keeping good time for him
and then for her

she says she knows I will
need a watch to get to class
we hug and she gets in

starts the car
eases into traffic
no wave

the metal of the back of the watch

is smooth to my thumb
and it keeps for a moment
a warmth from her skin.

She Leads Me

She leads me to the place under the trees
where her father years ago
fell dead

beside the buzz saw,
the broken blade in his throat.
Spot of earth where he lay

when she hurried to the grove and saw him.
Will you stay with the body? someone asked her,
and she did.

She knelt beside him, laid her apron over his face.
The body dressed in chore clothes,
layers of shirts, heavy coat, no gloves,

the better to guide the wood
to the blade. The body
needing work, needing cattle,

a horse to ride, a barn to build,
as if work were food and drink:
lift this, carry this, never put it down.

The body, marvelous when bending,
beautiful kneeling, hammering,
delicate the movement, the dance.

Her hands on my shoulders, she turns me to face her.
You can always—she tells me,

her lips pursing and flexing, her teeth square and gray—

you can always do what you have to do.

Desert Winter Baby

The two of them had a hundred days
before my father shipped out

he had his orders he had his uniform
I slept afternoons

in a basket
on their sunny balcony

desert air
stirring the palm tree

they had a hundred nights
their window open, their moon above the fence

Mewling or sleeping
I was part of what they had

they had the dark
the breeze the blanket

warm strong breath
their arms, their arms.

Those Pieces We Carry

My mother carried a leather purse, stashed it
under her arm, brought it out when needed

like the dry cough she used
in a roomful of strangers, a church, any

uncomfortable place. She had a dog, Moose,
the first of several Chihuahuas in the dynasty.

Moose's toenails ticked down the hall,
his ears up as if to help him fly,

hind half wagging, eyes shining.
My mother was eager

but afraid, sure she'd be stepped on.
She needed protection and warmth,

sitting up in the hospital bed,
her hands empty. *I had a little dog where is it*

she asked me. I had the advantage of health
and organized answers.

I sat in a chair beside her bed
and explained everything.

Jennie Held My Mother

I heard my mother
thrashing in her bed and I thought

This is it, she's going now, she's going—
but she didn't go. Some part of her
waited the night. The next morning

my sister arrived,
sat on the bed,
and held Mom on her lap,

not enfolding face to face
but Pietà-like,
with Mom facing away

and Jennie looking off into distance.
It was past the time of talking.
My mother's arms

churned wildly.
These two had had
the most trouble,

the most anger.
It seemed to be my mother's work
to swing her skinny bare white arms

as if she were a newborn who
no longer had the womb wall around her,

and my sister's work:
to allow reaching and thrashing
and, for as long as needed, to hold.

How to Live After Your Mother Leaves You

Wave your opinion like a flag
when talking to anyone at your table,

overshooting from afar and sideways.
Love especially the young.
Describe for them what they will

run into, roaming the extravagant
piebald jungle out there.

Be a Marco Polo come back
with your caravan and baggage

from the place they are longing for.
Point them to it, though you have
only dreamed its trees and fountains.

How I Left You

I walked to the river and stood
on the bridge at sundown

long strings of cranes
wavered toward me

long knotted strings
and the trilling of thousands

I went as a cheetah I left
home I went as a hawk I could see you

below I went as a seed from this
world each time I went out I

swallowed you you swallowed me
sleek in my gorgeous spots

I went as the milky way I overflow
I hide in my glorious coat.

II.

THROUGH THIS THIN WALL

didn't the girl in the headlines pray oh god with all her

strength when she realized her abductor was going to rape and kill
her didn't she pray

earnestly and the women casting off their three-inch heels as
they walked

down the stairs of the towers, didn't they pray stairway by stairway
stepping on or

over the shoes of others floor by floor praying and still the towers fell
and the dust rose,

the dust of prayers rose.

Bad News Good News

I was at a camp in the country,
you were home in the city,
and bad news had come to you.

You texted me as I sat
with others around a campfire.
It had been a test you and I

hadn't taken seriously,
hadn't worried about.
You texted the bad news word

cancer. I read it in that circle
around the fire. There was
singing and laughter to my right and left

and there was that word on the screen.
I tried to text back but,
as often happened in that county,

my reply would not send, so I went to higher ground.
I stood on a hill above the river and sent you
the most beautiful words I could manage,

put them together, each following each. Under
Ursa Major, Polaris, Cassiopeia, a space station flashing,
I said what had been said

many times, important times, foolish times:
those words soft-bodied humans say when the news is bad.

The *I love you* we wrap around our

need and hurl at the cosmos: Take this, you heartless
nothing and everything, take this.
I chose words to fling into the dark toward you

while the gray-robed coyote came out of hiding
and the badger wandered the unlit hill
and the lark rested herself in tall grasses;

I sent the most necessary syllables
we have, after all this time the ones we want to hear:
I said *Home*, I said *Love*, I said *Tomorrow*.

Pink to Purple

> *Even in Kyoto*
> *Hearing the cuckoo's cry*
> *I long for Kyoto*
>
> —Matsuo Bashō

It is not complicated. I am at the window
watching the mountains turn their brief pink.

They will become purple
in a minute. So truncated

our time. When you speak,
I don't

listen. The night is made
simple by the curve of the moon. The adobe wall

will surround our sand and cactus in the dark.
I cannot be your everything, you with your feet

up, your fuzzy socks, your secret ancient argument.
Sometimes the great horned owl

calls from the neighbor's pole and it is
the owl's note

that voices my yearning. Even in
happiness I long for happiness.

This Morning When the Mudflats Appear

This morning when the mudflats appear
under the tilted stranded boats,
I am thinking of how I try to live

with you, and live with my needs,
or even know what they are.
When I was a child, I stood below

while a carpenter constructed
the upper level of a house; he
moved about in the second story

before it had floors, stepping
on the rafters to cross the rooms
that were taking shape.

Your halt, reversal,
pause, to which
I pay too much attention. Your

important silences. You let your
body hurt, make it hurt, make it pay,
as if it were me.

The tide will come back and the gulls
will glide on invisible roads above the water,
roads they see or make.

Waking Up at Home on New Year's Day

Here in these rooms
our shortcomings, our ache,

our package deals. Here the shoes in a row,
the overflow sweaters.

What we have is photos:
her stance in her boots,

the flair of her shoulders,
his thin body, what he does with his

arms, just like his father.
Here we take up our

hope and fluff it and rest it.
The wind moans around the windows

in the same notes it used at
the windows of the grandmothers.

Let me become the stubborn quail, sending out
my questions in the dark.

Thanksgiving for Two

The adults we call our children will not be arriving
with their children in tow for Thanksgiving.
We must make our feast ourselves,

slice our half-ham, indulge, fill our plates,
potatoes and green beans
carried to our table near the window.

We are the feast, plenty of years,
arguments. The whole bundle of it
rolls out like a white tablecloth. We wanted

to be good company for one another.
Little did we know that first picnic
how this would go. Your hair was heavy,

mine long and easy; we climbed a bluff
to look over a storybook plain. We chose
our spot as high as we could, to see

the river and the checkerboard fields.
What we didn't see was this day, in
our pajamas if we want to,

wrinkled hands strong, good wine
in cheap glasses, toasting
whatever's next,

the decades of side-by-side,
our great good luck.

We Disagree

Your chin took on that particular jut
I would come to know,

white stone above the innocent plaid
of your collar. You were

mashing the potatoes, we had your parents
coming for dinner, I was making gravy, had

taken off my blouse to prevent spots. I,
in a black bra and red apron, you in

strength and righteousness. We were
interesting, arguing. You

manhandled the pot of potatoes,
threw in a slab of butter, poured in milk.

You beat the bejesus out of those spuds,
the beater clacking

with every stroke. *Beat beat beat,*
your biceps fine, rounded, a vein

visible under the skin, your face
stern above the potatoes. I whisked the

roux in the cast iron skillet, turned up
the heat. It was impasse

but I knew they'd be here any minute
and we had to be a happy couple

so I poured in lots of broth
and stirred like my grandmother

to make everything smooth
in time to put my shirt back on.

The Print the Whales Make

You and I on the boat notice
the print the whales leave,
the huge ring their diving draws
for a time on the surface.
Is it like that when we
lose one another? Don't
know, can't. But
I want to believe
when we can no longer
walk across a room
for a hug, can no longer
step into the arms of the other,
there will be this:
some trace that stays
while the great body
remains below out of sight,
dark mammoth shadow
flick of flipper
body of delight
diving deep.

The Frost That Will Crack Our Bones

> *Think of the frost*
> *that will crack our bones eventually.*
> —Tom Hennen

Let me think of the gray-green weed that will
grow on the grave above the casket.

Let me think of how I ruined
Christmas Eve one year when I would not

let slide what you said,
again. I was wearing

the blue robe you gave, wearing it
over my sweater and jeans, my feet

in the new slippers for the first
of thousands of times. I wish I had walked

into the yard to look at the stars, Pleiades perhaps,
that cold cluster of lights far from the warm

fragrant stubborn righteous vindicated
folds and limbs and symmetry of our selves.

Perhaps you would have followed me or
I would have called you to look at what is

so very distant and in that manner—that
or some other ploy—I could have

maneuvered you close to me,
the heat and welcome of your body.

Window

In the barn, a square opening to the loft,
where you spread a quilt,
a membrane over hay.

You heavy on me,
sounds under me, under the quilt
the breaking

of the dry stems.
Smell of semen, smell of alfalfa,
and, below, thud of hooves

of the restless horse in his stall.
I thought that opening,
that turning in hay,

would change everything.
I stood at a window,
coffee cup in hand,

window keeping the town
outside and the furniture of my life
inside: mismatched couches, chairs.

Window my body made
for the child to squeeze through,
sleep I tried to wake from

to see his birth,
window of anesthesia closing.

Window of notebook: how it

frames what I begin to know,
how it lets me almost say what I've
wanted to say. Window of

nightmare: I stand in a house
at the bottom of the ocean,
window ready,

water waiting.
Window opening—
not now, not yet.

Invisible

We could see no one but ourselves;
we were in love, which made us invisible,
made my car invisible, parked all night

around the corner in the neighborhood.
And made me invisible the next morning
when we drove to breakfast, laughing,

you and I, so sure that Frank and Donna
next door, look as hard as they might,
couldn't see me in the passenger seat,

slid down, hiding, as you backed
out of your garage. Oh, you were gorgeous,
laughing. Young, taut, tanned.

I had my hush-hush
vantage point, below eye level
in your sleek new who-cares car.

Tonight Two Butterflies

Tonight two butterflies in the backyard
are racing, no trace of sedate flutter,
rather fast figure-eights the width of the lawn,
again and again crisscrossing the space before me.
I sit alone on the patio, single observer of butterflies zipping.
Who will believe me in the morning? This racing and chasing
they do together, as if they have routes they must
speed up to finish, must complete before
heavy rain fills the air and prevents them
so they dash, traverse the distance,
such velocity for these mere dots
and now the requisite up-stroke,
the rise, the mountain, the cliff of the ash tree
and down, quick,
the marvelous twirl
one around the other
like binary stars or
children holding hands, spinning—
minute dancers, minute orbits,
repeat repeat:
headlong dash,
climb, descend, twirl.
I am a wide-eyed witness to a great boogie,
salsa, marathon, life, weightless craziness—
what body can bear this spinning, this intricate chase?—
made more marvelous because so small, so fierce—
night comes, the rain comes,
but first two atoms in tandem
careen across a vast plain.

I Am One of Those Who Should Have Been Swans

I should have been voiceless;
what grief that would save:

a certain hush when I have said
what should not have been mentioned,

the mistake hangs in the room,
a sour stink, and everyone

dreads what else I might say.
Better if on half-moon nights

I'd float on the lake, a pale silent flower,
my neck a long curve

above the box of my body,
my eye a black unseeing pearl.

No.

Wings and box, open.
Eye and beak, open.

I want a world where
even the silenced can sing.

Where Orion Has Got To

Sleepless, I wrap in a quilt and walk out
to see where Orion has got to.

It's that time between
the day that was

and the day that will be. Orion lay
last night on his back in the east. Now

he's moved, shoulders and sword
glistening, around to a place

in the western sky.
Someone I love pulls on his watch cap

and steps across a threshold,
a beginning, a divide.

The mist of his breath freezes white on his lashes,
His stride sounds on the hard path.

To the Woman Having Sex in the Next Room

Stranger making moan again at two in the morning, your bed is
bumping my paper-thin wall. For a while you were talking: his voice
the tenor and your voice a little brook over stones. Oh isn't it fine, yes,
to have this man so interested in what you say. Woman moaning and
bucking and jumping next door, I wish you much happiness, even
more than you presently have, though you may be thinking you have
plenty. May I project this upon you?— you will find something to fill
your yearning and you will find

nothing to fill it. You may be thinking at last the yearning will stop,
that you have found a way and perhaps even a *one* to stop its ache.
You have not. I'm projecting. You yearn, you have yearned, you will
have yearned. The man I took my clothes off for and waited for, I
don't think he yearns now or ever did for what I wanted—not even I
know exactly what I wanted. I know I *wanted*

also in the sense of *lacked*. I found myself wanting and went about
in my lost-puppy way to fix it. My mother saw it and couldn't help
me, was still trying to figure out her own unhappiness. Happiness is
a tricky thing, you of the superb orgasm. At least you seem to have
that, which I did not and therefore faulted myself and faked it or
maybe you are just a better, noisier faker. I feel a kinship with you
though you may be very

unlike what I imagine. Imagination: that which doesn't leave when
the smooth skin of youth goes. When the slender waist and the
muscle tone leave, when the other gets up and puts clothes on and
goes to work or goes to pee or goes to smoke or goes to find firmer
flesh. Was it bitterness that said that? I am at a distance looking back
and yet close, just next door. In that first bed I threw away much

when I threw down my clothing. But aren't those moans

all about being alive? I don't want you to stop, just as I didn't wish
you to start. Look, I'll turn on the light and keep writing you,
writing myself. I know little about you and I know little about me.
The softness that overlays our bones at 20. I said *our,* as if we share.
I wanted to be wanted. Do we share that? Stranger beyond this
cracker-thin division, moaning to joys of the body, scary and good,
are we not corks carried in a current of wanting?

Not Exactly a Holiday

I would like to tell how my sister and I
clown around while we get the turkey ready.
I'd like to show how she makes the dressing

in her cross-eyed imitation of a TV chef,
especially her sound effects, especially when
she mixes with both hands. My laughter and her

gummy-handed threats. I'd like to
show the huge pale body of the turkey
in a sink full of cold water and how

she and I wrestle the bird to dry land,
pat it with towels, and stuff it with stuffing.
I'd like you to hear how we finish one another's

jokes, and everything is to howl at. The bumps
on the skin of the tail end of the turkey.
The specter of food poisoning

and the yearly dilemma of
how hot, how long, whether 'tis nobler to tent
or not to tent. I'd like to, but that happiness

happened only once or something like it
almost happened once. What happened
is that we stood on the front step of my house

where she told me how wrong I was,
trying to pretend we were OK,

that if I wanted to play dumb,

it was fine with her.
She is forever in her car, driving away,
turning the last corner, and I

stand, my arms vacant,
an open-handed truth branding
the side of my ignorant face.

III.

BRIGHT KITE OVER THE HORIZON

She Tells Her Child of the Assassination

In November of 1963, you
were all the center of my days
and when I heard on TV

Kennedy had been shot,
I wrapped you in your blue
blanket and walked for miles (I was

strong then), carrying you
on sidewalks in the middle
of a country stunned by rapid-fire

bulletins. It was
pink Chanel suit, brain matter,
film loop, Walter Cronkite—

but I had your sweet-
smelling head close to my lips
and I walked 40th Street. The leaves

broke and scattered under my feet.
I passed the blank faces of doors and windows,
the news spreading dark over the lawns.

Local Boy Taken

His mother receives a folded flag.
Somebody holds a sign that says *Thank You.*

Somebody says he was a jokester.
Somebody says his favorite trick

was to run across the room and fall down
as though he hit an imaginary clothesline.

He did this trick in a department store
in the section where his brother was working.

He ran, pretended to hit the clothesline,
fell down.

His sergeant says he volunteered for duties
like cleaning the floor with a toothbrush.
Somebody says that was just how he was.

Somebody says he was a natural with a wrench,
and he could dunk a basketball.
Once he shattered the backboard.

Those assembled at the cemetery
stand through a round of rifle shots.

He ran across the room.
He ran across the room
and fell down.

My Son with Ghosts

The ancestors, shadowy forms,
line up and overlap behind him. He is

trying to build a house and
they know how to build

only the house they were given.
They hold the board as he hammers

or they are the arm bringing
the hammer down or they

sabotage, as they were sabotaged,
pulling the board away. He bends

to pick up the fallen
nail and begin again.

Let High Noon Enter

You are in that hour between innocence
and business, your hair thicker

to the hand than ever again, the light
shining so your eyes are more blue

than blue really is, the earnest beauty of one
always at home in snow, like the cave you

dug into a drift, the slippery
doorway into it, you, red-cheeked, digging

with your hands. I keep you in that
red parka of innocence though you grow

away, up nights, sleeping days.
Everything I did, you magnify. I don't want

details, can't know them, must let you
go like a bright kite over the horizon. Let

high noon enter, let happen what will happen,
and I keep that image of you in snow:

red coat, wet mittens, no cap, wolf-pup eyes,
emerging from your den.

For My Daughter

When they laid you on my belly
and cut the cord
and wrapped you and gave you
to my arms, I looked into the face
I already loved. The cheekbones,
the nose, the deep place
the eyes opened to. I thought
then this is the one I must teach,
must shape and nurture.
I was sure I should. How was I
to know you would become
the one to show me
how kindness walks in the world?
Some days the daughter
is the mother,
is the hand that reaches
out over the pond, sprinkling
nourishment on the water.
Some days I am the lucky koi,
rising from below, opening
the circle of my mouth to take it in.

Last Day of Kindergarten

In the photograph
the boy is ecstatic,
set free, a young king,
everything ahead of him.
There is nothing he can't have
if he wants it and he wants it,
as does his friend beside him.
They are ready now to ride off
together and slay dragons,
rescue the world. It's all here
in the park after the last bell;
it's here in the green summer
they have been released to.
It's here in their manhood.
They've only finished kindergarten
but they understand freedom
and friendship. They're on top
of the picnic table, they're on top
of the world in their tennis shoes,
they have raised their arms,
they are such men as could
raise continents; they have
survived. Look how their
fingers reach the sky
and their legs are sure as
horses. Their bodies
will forever do anything they ask.

Earth from Saturn

The earth from Saturn
is a pale blue orb
and you'd have to squint

to see the garbage truck
working its way down my street.
From across the galaxy,

or even from across town,
you'd have to imagine me
at the window, a stick figure

with curly hair, and a whole
sunny earthbound green-as-
grass day ahead of me.

Feeling Pretty Religious

I was standing on the patio
shortly after daybreak, listening

to the rain begin on the grass,
listening to one hidden bird

whistling her two notes:
See me. See me.

That's what I
like about jealousy,

the way it slows you down
and makes you curious. How can

I sing like that? I stand
in my pajamas and bathrobe,

underemployed, looking at
the green ash in its old age

and the hula hoop a child left
hanging there, as high as she could reach.

Margit, Age 24, Treblinka

Near Warsaw, 1942

Margit stands, naked, with others,
on the lip of the ditch,

the ditch dug for her,
for them.

If she looked up, she could see a row of soldiers,
a row of rifles, ready.

She looks at the cold freckled skin of her arms;
she has crossed them in front of her.

Across the ditch:
a soldier in a line of soldiers.

His shape, his shoulder, his rifle.

Her toes
in the fresh dirt.

Draw What Is There

In art class, the instructor says
Draw your hand—not an idea of hand

but what is really there.
My pencil scratches over paper,

telling the truth. Wrinkles.
Crookedness and bulges.

I let the ring fall to the side,
as it often does, let the tunneling

veins go where they have to go,
but left out is this:

the day I pulled your hair,
my son,

when you broke something.
It was too much, all of it.

Not the green plastic
forgettable trifle you broke;

I mean my work, my union with your father.
It was too much and it was too little

and you were there, young and perfect
and close by my hand. You say

you don't remember
so I don't mention it again

but I remember and
have not let it go.

Let me turn my hand over, watch
the ends of the fingers catch light,

notice that knuckles are only creases
over the bones that do the work.

Let me see what is
in front of me, opening and closing.

Let what I did and failed to do
drop like a leaf from my hand.

NOTES

Page 18, title inspired by the line "It does not have to be worth the dying" from "Let Me Tell You" by Miller Williams, from *Living on the Surface: New and Selected Poems* (Louisiana State University Press, 1989)

Page 52, title inspired by the line "There are girls who should have been swans" in "After Whistler" by Lisel Mueller, from *Alive Together: New and Selected Poems* (Louisiana State University Press, 1996)

Page 62, title inspired by the line "Let high noon enter" in "Little Girl, My String Bean, My Lovely Woman" by Anne Sexton, from *Selected Poems of Anne Sexton* (Houghton Mifflin Company, 1988)

ACKNOWLEDGMENTS

"Thanksgiving for Two," *American Life in Poetry*

"She Leads Me," *Becoming: What Makes a Woman*

"Draw What Is There" and "Let High Noon Enter," *burntdistrict*

"Hands" and "I Meant to Write of My Sister's Pain," *The Fourth River*

"I Have Nothing to Say About Fire" and "Margit, Age 24, Treblinka,"
    Malala: Poems for Malala Yousafzai

"She Gives Me the Watch off Her Arm," *Nimrod*

"Bad News Good News," *PoetryMagazine.com*

"The Story, Part of It," *Rattle.com*

CPSIA information can be obtained
at www.ICGtesting.com
Printed in the USA
FSOW04n0355090617
34874FS

9 781935 218395